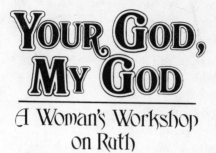

YOUR GOD, MY GOD

A Woman's Workshop on Ruth

Books in this series—

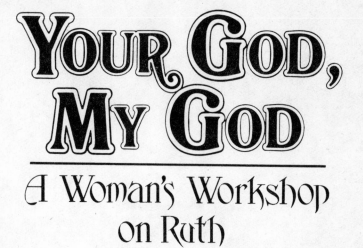

YOUR GOD, MY GOD

A Woman's Workshop on Ruth

Leader's Manual

Anne Wilcox

Lamplighter Books Grand Rapids, Michigan
Zondervan Publishing House

Your God, My God
Copyright © 1985 by The Zondervan Corporation
Grand Rapids, Michigan

Library of Congress Cataloging in Publication Data
Wilcox, Anne.
    Your God, my God.
    Bibliography: p.
    1. Bible. O.T. Ruth—Study. 2. Bible. O.T. Ruth—Criticism, interpretation, etc.
I. Title.
BS1315.5.W55   1985   222'.3506   85-716
ISBN 0-310-44691-0

Edited by Kin Millen and Janet Kobobel

Printed in the United States of America

85 86 87 88 89 90 / 10 9 8 7 6 5 4 3 2 1

To
Coralie Wilcox
my mother-in-law
and dear friend

CONTENTS

PREFACE

You can use this Bible study manual to increase your comprehension of the Book of Ruth, and to facilitate personal interaction with its message. The lessons are designed for home Bible studies, small discussion groups, or personal study. Each lesson contains questions, charts, and projects designed for creative observations, careful interpretations, and contemporary applications. Study skills transferable to other narrative portions of the Bible are taught through this workshop, but its primary focus is to impart skills for living faithfully in a faithless age.

Since Ruth comprises an ancient Jewish story, the first four chapters of this study are written to help our contemporary minds explore the cultural and historical influences Ruth experienced three thousand years ago. She gleaned wheat by hand. Today we gather it in stereo-equipped combines. Despite the technological differences of our eras, Ruth faced the same moral and spiritual decisions that confront us today.

In this study, you will also become acquainted with Boaz, whose obedience surpasses the letter of the Law· and expresses the true spirit of God's commands. As you watch Naomi, you will see the struggles and choices of a woman passing through seasons of heartache and seasons of blessing. As each character is brought into sharper focus through your study, you will see the hope they give us for living godly lives in the midst of a godless age.

Throughout the Book of Ruth, you will observe a God who is intimately at work in the lives of all who respond to Him by faith. You will see that though He allows loss and heartache to touch His people, He has not lost control.

The final verses of Ruth testify to His sovereign control of the world's history. To Israel these verses spoke of the national hope that came through King David's leadership. To us the verses speak of the Davidic line through which the world's Savior has come.

May you embrace God wholeheartedly as Ruth did, and may the next generation observe and say, "Your God Shall Be My God!"

ACKNOWLEDGMENTS

My first in-depth study of the Book of Ruth began while team-teaching a Bible study with D.D. Mitchell. I thank her for critiquing the manuscript and praying it to completion. Her mastery of both the Scriptures and the English language have made an invaluable contribution to this study.

I am deeply grateful for the enthusiastic support of Dr. Ronald B. Allen. His research suggestions and teaching materials have added new dimensions to my understanding of this Hebrew story.

Without Kin Millen, *A Woman's Workshop on Ruth* would still be in the raw. In the middle of the project he graciously provided professional advice and assistance. Through the final rigors of editing his encouragement and wit made the process not only tolerable but also completely enjoyable.

Many times in the final stages of a book the end seems impossible to achieve. At one of those moments, Jennifer

Batts offered to help with the typing. Without her ministry, the deadline would still be unmet.

My deepest thanks goes to my supportive family. My husband graciously accepted my marriage to the typewriter during many hours of research and writing. My parents, Dick and Dorothy Hagerman, generously provided opportunities to continue my education in writing and my parents-in-law, Cliff and Coralie Wilcox, volunteered hours of grandparenting for two-year-old Jaime as I worked to meet deadlines.

INSTRUCTIONS FOR LEADERS

Objectives

Each chapter of the leader's manual begins with goals for the lesson. These objectives reflect a progression of study from observation to interpretation to application. Only after carefully observing Scripture can we make skillful interpretations, and only after skillfully interpreting can we begin to make appropriate applications to our lives. This sequence is an integral part of each lesson and should be reinforced during the discussion time.

Background Material

Following the objectives, background material is included. If the passage under consideration contains words or customs foreign to present-day understanding, these items are defined under "Cultural Definitions." The rest of the background material may be used as added information during the discussion time. It may also be used for brief introductory remarks as you open your study each week.

Questions

Each question from the student manual is reproduced in the leader's materials. Additional research is added to some questions as well as ideas for directing the discussion.

Near the application portion of the lessons you will notice questions designated by an asterisk. These are marked for personal meditation and self-examination. They are designed to encourage individual response to God. You may decide to eliminate these questions from the group discussion because of their personal nature. The transparency and trust within your group should be factors in your decision.

Preparation Ideas

Review the objectives for all twelve lessons. This will provide you with an overview of the study and the emphasis of each lesson. After this quick overview, complete the first lesson in the student manual without consulting the leader's manual. Then check the leader's manual for additional information and group ideas.

At the end of each lesson, the leader's manual contains thoughts on how specific prayer can be used to reinforce the study. Responding to God explicitly helps to personalize the teaching of each lesson and will also help give purpose and direction to your group prayer.

As a matter of fact, prayer is the best way to begin as you prepare your first lesson. . .

1

DOING YOUR OWN THING IN ANTIQUITY

Objectives

1. To become familiar with the historical setting of the Book of Ruth.
2. To evaluate the spiritual mood of the time period.
3. To consider how one might influence the spiritual tenor of our own time.

Like a stage crew painting the backdrop for a play, your study group will recreate the historical setting for the Book of Ruth. In this first lesson, you will closely examine Israel's period of the judges. A thorough understanding of the people's fickle spirituality in this era provides a contrast to Ruth's sacrificial commitment. The attitudes of that day parallel with the attitudes of our present age, showing that a faith like Ruth's is possible in today's culture. This simple but profound narrative also demonstrates how one woman's faith in the living God can influence the course of history.

15

Background

This period of Israel's history begins after the death of the great warrior Joshua. He and his contemporaries were eyewitnesses to God's glorious victories as He brought His people into the Promised Land. Despite their experiences, they died without effectively communicating their faith to the next generation.

In the beginning of the Book of Judges, a new age appears of people who are unfamiliar with the Lord. They are not experiencing His works firsthand, and they are not obeying His commands. They have allowed their relationship with God to be buried with their fathers. Because of this spiritual regression, the new generation cannot drive the rest of the foreigners from their inherited land. Instead, the Israelites have allowed themselves to be influenced by these foreign nations by embracing their idolatry.

Despite their rebellion, God does not abandon them. He continues to express His love through discipline. Over and over He judges their actions by letting other nations rule them. In response to this discipline, the Israelites cry out for forgiveness and mercy. Each time, their gracious God responds by sending a judge to save them from their oppression.

After each intervention, peace and safety is enjoyed in the land. All too soon, however, the people forget God's mercy and indulge in sin once again. This cycle of sin, discipline, salvation, and rest is repeated seven times through the Book of Judges and covers approximately three hundred years.

In the midst of this spasmodic spirituality, the story of Ruth emerges as a stark contrast. Ruth's consistent faithfulness runs counter to the behavior of her culture. She refuses to serve the gods of her own Moabite people but embraces the true God with all her heart. In both hardship and blessing, she remains faithful to God and His people.

1. *The major periods of Israel's history can be illustrated in the following table. Read Ruth 1:1 and circle the historical period that provides the background for this narrative.*

The period of the judges should be circled on the table in the student's manual. You may wish to share this graphic description of the judges with your study group:

> The Book of Ruth should be read in the context of the period of the judges (Ruth 1:1). The judges did not render judicial verdicts; they executed judgment as the charismatic deliverers of the people of God in times of distress. They were the Matt Dillons of the Old Testament.
>
> —Dr. Ronald B. Allen
> Professor of Old Testament
> Language and Exegesis at
> Western Conservative
> Baptist Seminary

2. *The events of this period of history are recorded for us in the Book of Judges. Judges 2:16–19 summarizes this era's spiritual tenor. As you read the passage below: a) underline the people's actions and attitudes; b) circle God's actions and attitudes.*

This exercise allows your study group to see the people's inconsistent faith and allegiance and God's constant compassion. It will help illustrate God's strong discipline and His gracious mercy despite Israel's disobedience.

3. *What word or phrase would you use to describe the Israelites' hearts during the period of the judges?*

Singleness of heart certainly did not characterize the

people of this era. They would better be described by the words "forgetful," "compromising," and "disobedient."

4. *List the attributes God expressed during these generations.*

Two of God's attributes clearly seen during this period are His justice and His love. His justice is expressed as He allows other nations to rule His people in punishment for their disobedience. His faithful love is expressed as He continually responds to His oppressed people's cries and is moved to save them again and again. This pattern of chastisement followed by mercy illustrates a compassionate, holy God.

5. *Many years before the judges, warnings against spiritual forgetfulness were given by God through His spokesman Moses. Compare the instructions in Deuteronomy 6:1–9 with the appraisal of the first generation in the era of judges (Judges 2:10). Who was to blame for this spiritual drought?*

Under Joshua's leadership, the Israelites had seen God intervene many times on their behalf to secure the Promised Land from the Canaanites. But within their own households, they failed to transfer the reality of God and their own religious experience to their children. Neither did this younger generation respond to the truth that was available to them. Between incompetent transferal of truth and unresponsiveness to God, both generations carry the blame for the absence of commitment to God.

In our own generation, we need to examine the accuracy and authenticity of our communication about God to our families and to others we influence. We also need to examine our practical demonstration of these messages. Are we modeling truth or merely speaking it? The next generation will be influenced by what we have believed and how we have lived, yet they cannot live on our spiritual strength. They must enter into their *own* living experience with God.

6. *In your own words, rewrite the epitaph for this historical period found in Judges 21:25.*

The New International Version translates the end of this verse, "everyone did as he saw fit." The New American Standard translates this section, "everyone did what was right in his own eyes." The Living Bible paraphrases it as "every man did whatever he thought was right."

7. *The entire Book of Ruth could easily fit on the daily newspaper's front page. Read the book in one sitting. When you finish, create an appropriate epitaph for Ruth's life.*

Example of epitaph:

> Ruth the Moabitess, a woman who did not do what was right in her own eyes, but who chose what was right before God and transferred godliness to the next generation.

8. *What epitaph would you give your generation?*

In many ways, the period of the judges resembles our era, and the same epitaph could apply. It could be phrased like this:

> Here lies the generation that did
> what was right in its own eyes,
> and did it faster than any generation
> had ever done it before.

9. *Analyze an opinion you have recently heard concerning a contemporary moral issue by answering the following questions:*

   a. *What general philosophy of life does this opinion reflect?*

b. *What standards govern the life of the person holding this opinion?*

To prepare for this discussion, select a moral issue being discussed in the media and become conversant with the various opinions. Be prepared to explain all sides of the issue to illustrate how people selectively use data to form opinions of convenience and self-justification. The question is designed to heighten awareness of contemporary thinking regarding morality.

10. *Does one individual have any hope for influencing society today? Before answering this question, try the following project:*

a. *List current philosophies or situations that you feel contradict God's moral laws.*

Carefully evaluate the examples your group shares. See if the women can use Scripture to show whether or not the issue they share violates God's moral will. Be sure the Scripture they use is in context and that the whole counsel of God's Word agrees with their conclusions. Be certain they are taking a stand on a timeless truth and not just an idea they learned in a seminar, a tradition they hold sacred, or a conviction unique to a particular denomination. We need to be discerning women in these times, knowing when to embrace issues without compromise and when to welcome diversity of opinion. We must be sure we are not equating personal notions with the Word of God. Skillful expression of His truth to our world is desperately needed.

b. *Look over the options below. Choose one action you can accomplish this week to influence change in one of the areas you listed.*

By your own example, encourage the women to choose an action to express their convictions from the options listed in the student manual. You may want to begin your next study time by allowing the group to share the joys and frustrations of its attempts to influence others. Personal accountability is a critical element for the growth of any study group. Enjoy sharing with one another actions that express desire to change your moment of history.

*11. *Look back at the epitaph you wrote for your generation. What do you wish the epitaph would say? Ask the Lord to use you in bringing about the change you desire for your generation and for the ones to follow.*

Try to end your study time with conversational prayer, focusing on the response to this last question. Ask the women to express their desired changes for their generation in prayer. Then give them opportunity to express their commitment to participate in these changes. End the prayer time with praise and acknowledgment of God's sovereign role in our lives and in all of history.

---

*These questions throughout the book are for personal thought and reflection.

2

CROSS-CULTURAL ADJUSTMENTS

Objectives

1. To understand the tension between Ruth's Moabite heritage and the Israelite culture she chose to adopt.
2. To evaluate the acceptance Ruth received from God and His people.
3. To begin to model God's standard of acceptance as we relate to others.

Background

While studying the interactions between Moab and Israel, it helps to identify certain Moabite events that have major significance in the Old Testament stream of redemptive history. The table on the next page gives the chronology of events that affected both countries. (Most dates are approximate.)

Dates	Moabite And Israelite Events Intertwined	Reference
2141 B.C.	God promises Abraham a son through Sarah.	Gen. 18
	Sodom and Gomorrah are destroyed.	Gen. 19
	Abraham's nephew, Lot, escapes from Sodom and Gomorrah.	Gen. 19
	Lot's eldest daughter conceives a child through incest. The baby boy who is born is named, "Moab", meaning from my father.	Gen. 19
	The history of the Patriarchs of Israel is recorded. (Abraham, Isaac, Jacob, Joseph)	Gen. 12–50
1804 B.C.	Joseph and his generation dies.	Exod. 1
	Hardship and bondage begin for the people of Israel.	Exod. 1
	Moses is born.	Exod. 2
	The Exodus from Egypt is accomplished.	Exod. 12
	Moab is mentioned in the victory song of Moses.	Exod. 15
April 1, 1444 B.C.	The Tabernacle is completed.	Exod. 40
	Worship and sacrificial instructions are given to the nation of Israel.	Leviticus
May 1, 1444 B.C.	The first census of Israel is taken.	Num. 1
	Battles rage between Israel and the surrounding nations.	Num. 21
	Moab is terrified at the victories of Israel.	Num. 22
	Balak, king of Moab, sends for the prophet Balaam in hopes of bringing a curse upon the nation of Israel, but Balaam speaks blessings toward Israel and destruction towards Moab.	Num. 22–24
	Israel's last encampment before crossing the Jordan was at Shittim within the old Moabite boundaries. During this stay, the Moabite women invited Israelite men to join in their worship celebrations to	Num. 25:1–3

Dates	Moabite And Israelite Events Intertwined	Reference
	pagan gods. Immorality was practiced and God's anger was expressed.	
Feb. 1, 1405 B.C.	The last sermons of Moses are spoken to the people.	Deut. 1:5
	Moses reminds the Israelites of the Lord's prohibition against provoking the *Moabites*. Because *Moab* is related to Israel through Lot's relationship to Abraham, God has designated a certain area of land for their use. Israel is not to bother them.	Deut. 2:9
	Moab is excluded from the assembly of the Lord. The Israelites are instructed not to seek peace or good relations with the *Moabite* people.	Deut. 23:3
March 1405 B.C.	Moses dies and is buried in the geographic area called the *Plains of Moab*.	Deut. 34
	The Israelites enter the Promised Land.	Joshua
	The Lord, through Joshua, reminds His people of the victory over *Moab* during Balak's reign as king of *Moab*.	Josh. 24:9
1390 B.C.	Joshua and his generation dies.	Judg. 1
	The period of the judges begins.	Judg. 3
	In judgment of Israel's waywardness, God allows *Eglon, king of Moab,* to rule over His people for 18 years.	Judg. 3
1150? B.C.	The events in the book of Ruth take place.	Judg. 6?
1043 B.C.	The nation of Israel asks Samuel to give them a king. The kingdom era begins.	1 Sam. 8
1043 B.C.	Saul is anointed King of Israel.	1 Sam. 10
1011 B.C.	The Lord chooses David as king over Israel. David is the great-grandson of *Ruth* and Boaz.	1 Sam. 16

1. *Underline all the times in the Book of Ruth that the author mentions Moab or Ruth's identification with this country. How many references did you discover? Why do you think the author gives us this repetition?*

The Book of Ruth contains thirteen references to Moab and Moabitess. Several other sections refer to Ruth's homeland, her people, her foreign heritage, and her gods.

This narrative is a Hebrew story written for Hebrew readers. It ends with the genealogy of David, one of Israel's greatest kings. The surprising fact that the heroine is a foreigner should immediately attract the attention of patriotic Israelites. Other famous stories contained in the Old Testament generally feature Israeli heroes and heroines.

Through the author of Ruth, God is expressing something unique about His dealings with Gentiles. The author reminds us indirectly that Ruth's "blood–type" was unacceptable according to the letter of the Law. At the same time we are shown that her heart was above reproach according to the spirit of the Law. She may not have qualified as a child of God outwardly, but she definitely qualified inwardly. (Romans 2:28–29 expresses this concept in the New Testament.)

2. *Compare the origin of the Moabites (Genesis 19:27– 38) with the origin of the Israelites (Genesis 12:1–3). How do you suppose the Israelites felt about their distant cousins based on these beginnings?*

Knowing precisely the feelings of people in an age and culture far removed from our own is impossible. But if basic human nature has remained unchanged since the period of the judges, then we can safely make the following assumptions.

One of the nations began through a miraculous act of God. The other nation began with an embarrassing act of sexual misconduct—incest. The Israelites probably felt disdain toward the Moabites. The Moabites, on the other hand, might have jealously desired any chance to gain a superior position over Israel (Judges 11:17). Moab ruling over Israel during the period of the judges must have been a source of enthusiastic gloating for Moab (Judges 3:12–30).

3. *When Ruth married Mahlon, she was introduced to another religion. When she left Moab, she chose to adopt Naomi's God as her own. Investigate the religion Ruth was leaving. See if you can discover the names of her local gods and the activities involved in worshiping these Moabite deities. (Research helps are in the student manual.)*

Chemosh was the local deity of the Moabite people. His goddess-mate was Astarte. The name Chemosh means subduer, and his character was that of a savage war god. Astarte, a goddess of war, was also worshiped as the goddess of love and fertility.

Worship of Astarte included the baking of sacrificial cakes and the burning of incense. Worshiping Chemosh involved burnt sacrifices of bulls, rams, and even children. These tokens of worship were offered on rough stone altars on local hillsides.

4. *God gave Israel many foreign relations policies through His servant Moses. Deuteronomy 2:9 and 23:3–6 are instructions concerning the policies with Moab. Compare the instructions in Deuteronomy 23:3–6 with the words of Israel's elders found in Ruth 4:11–12.*

It is important to remember that the prohibitions God gave in Deuteronomy were based on Moab's previous mistreatment of Israel.

Instructions from Deut. 23:3–6	Blessings from Ruth 4:11–12
—no Moabite or his descendants can enter the assembly of the Lord.	—may God bless this Moabite woman the same way He blessed the famous mothers who built the nation of Israel
—don't seek peace or good relations with Moab as long as you live	—may this Moabite woman bring prosperity and prestige to you and your family

5. *How would you explain the contrast of the previous chart?*

Ruth had not mistreated God's people. Quite the opposite was true. She had sacrificed everything to care for Naomi's needs. The people of Bethlehem had carefully watched her and had concluded that she was a person with rare character qualities (Ruth 3:11). She had sincerely expressed her desire to make Naomi's people her people and Naomi's God her God.

The people of Bethlehem also had examples of other Gentile women who had been included in Israel's lineage. Tamar, mentioned in the elders' blessing, was a foreign woman who had continued the line of Judah. Rahab, the mother or grandmother of Boaz, was also a Gentile woman applauded for her faith and included as a mother of Israel.

In Ruth's case, the people of Bethlehem were seeing past national hostility to an individual who desired to believe in and serve the God they worshiped. Instead of violating God's instructions, the elders were graciously expressing the heart of God as they included among their people a Gentile woman who was wholly committed to the God of Israel.

6. *Judges 3:12–30 records a national conflict between Moab and Israel during the period of the judges. Because of this episode, what barriers might Ruth have encountered when she first arrived in Bethlehem?*

It is likely that some of the Bethlehemites' relatives had been killed when Eglon, King of Moab, conquered their country. As a result, hatred between the opposing sides of these recent wars could not be easily dismissed. The text indicates that this Moabite woman was not expecting kindness in her new culture (Ruth 2:10).

7. *Numbers 25:1–3 records a religious conflict between Moab and Israel. How do you think the Israelite women initially reacted to a Moabite woman in their midst?*

Fortunately, Ruth came to Bethlehem with Naomi, a respected member of the village. She told the people about this sacrificial daughter-in-law, but the women must have had some initial apprehensions. They may have felt protective toward their sons who might take an interest in this young, attractive foreigner. They also may have felt afraid that she would encourage the worship of her native gods.

8. *How would you explain the blessing and praise these women gave Ruth (Ruth 4:15)?*

The women who came to view the baby probably were Naomi's special friends, perhaps the same ones who wept when she left for Moab so many years ago. If so, they would have been the first ones to meet Naomi when she reentered Bethlehem with her Moabite daughter-in-law. They would have wept as Naomi asked to be called Mara and described the bitter events of the past years. As the weeks of the barley harvest progressed, they must have marveled at the love Ruth expressed to Naomi through commitment and hard work.

Any apprehensions they may have had about Ruth were proven false.

The Hebrew women's appraisal of Ruth's worth to Naomi is amazing because of the place usually given boys in comparison with girls in their culture. These women considered Ruth to be more valuable than seven sons. The number seven represented perfection, and the birth of sons was a sign of God's blessing. It took a remarkable foreigner to receive such adulation from Hebrew women.

9. *What cultures or groups of people struggle to find acceptance in your community? Why do you think the problem exists?*

In preparation for this question, clip articles from your local paper that give examples of acceptance or prejudice within your community. Ask the members of the group how they perceived the community when they were new to it.

10. *Are there certain cultural groups that you have difficulty relating to or accepting? Identify the reasons for your feelings.*

This question is designed to help individuals identify prejudices they may harbor. We find it difficult to look on the heart the way God does. If we begin to understand why we feel hesitancy or hostility toward a certain culture or background, it may help us begin to see people as God sees them. If we continue to harbor our prejudices, we will miss the "Ruths" who pass through our lives.

11. *Are there people in your own home whom you find hard to accept? Evaluate why you have difficulty relating to them. Are their personalities and attitudes different than yours or too much like yours? Must they accomplish certain achievements to gain your acceptance?*

Help the group realize what specific expectations they have of the people they live with. Unmet expectations are the most frequent causes of anger and frustration. Many times we miss the joy of seeing an individual develop because we will not let go of our demand that they must be a certain way or do certain things before we will accept them. This question needs to be answered personally and specifically.

12. *Analyze your feelings toward those in your church who have come to Christ out of a different background than your own or at a different time than your experience.*

When we become children of God, we join a family that has "one Lord, one faith, one baptism; one God and Father of all, who is over all and through all and in all" (Ephesians 4:5–6). However, as in every family, hurts and misunderstandings frequently arise.

Some answers to this question may be quite personal. If you want to discuss this idea, you could ask the group to name the key factors they feel contribute to maintaining unity in the body of Christ.

13. *In your opinion, what criteria must a person meet before being accepted by God?*

The answers to this question will help you assess the spiritual understanding of your group. Many people sincerely feel they can merit favor before God by other avenues than faith in Jesus Christ. It will provide a good opportunity to follow up those who do not personally know Christ as their Savior.

Give the group these two New Testament references for further study of personal acceptance by God: Ephesians 2:8–9, which expresses that our salvation is through faith; Hebrews 11:6, which says, "Without faith it is impossible to please God, because anyone who comes to him must believe that he exists and that he rewards those who earnestly seek him.''

14. *What does God's treatment of Ruth show you about His standards for acceptance?*

How thankful we can be that God doesn't judge people the way society does. We usually put our emphasis on appearance, personality, intellect, and prestige. He is a lover of the dispossessed. He is always moved by the needs of the desperate and the disadvantaged.

In a broad scope, God demonstrated through Ruth's life His love for Gentiles who respond to Him in faith. On an individual level, He expressed His priority on the attitude of the heart and His eagerness to respond to anyone who calls on Him.

*15. *Take time before God to compare your standards of acceptance of others with His standards. Prayerfully choose one person who came to mind as you worked on questions 9–12. List specific ways your criteria of acceptance can begin to resemble God's as you interact with this person.*

The answers and projects related to this meditation question may not be appropriate for group sharing. If discussion is to take place, be sure names are not mentioned.

You can conclude your study time with praise to God for His unconditional love and acceptance not only during Ruth's era but also today.

3

SCENES FROM A LOVE STORY

Objectives

1. To trace the story line of Ruth by using literary elements.
2. To become acquainted with the three main characters by evaluating their dialogues.
3. To self-evaluate personal character revealed through recent words and dialogues.
4. To discern the impact of the book's key message.

Background

Some of the major messages of the Book of Ruth are identified in question 14 of this lesson. Apart from these messages, this book also presents three themes found in most Old Testament books. These themes are:

1. A stranger in a strange land.
2. A lack of obedience equals a lack of blessing.

3. God is the sustainer of those who trust Him.

Woven through these themes is an expression of the importance of family relationships. Ruth's devotion to her mother-in-law and her commitment to the preservation of the family name are both praised. Boaz's actions contribute to this emphasis of familial responsibility as he willingly acts as kinsman-redeemer. The story's ending, a genealogy, emphasizes God's blessing through the family line.

Listed below are the elements that contribute to a well-designed plot (adapted from Leland Ryken's The Literature of the Bible). *Read through them. Identify the scenes from Ruth that represent each element.*

Elements of a Skillful Plot	Representative Scenes from Ruth
1. *Exposition*—background material that brings the reader up to date with the character's present circumstances.	1. The sojourn in Moab and the subsequent deaths.
2. *Inciting Force*—circumstances that get the story moving.	2. The journey back to Bethlehem in the Land of Promise.
3. *Rising Action*—interesting developments that progress the plot.	3. Boaz begins to show interest and concern over the plight of the two widows.
4. *Turning Point*—an entrance in the story of a possible solution to the existing conflicts.	4. Naomi has a plan to secure help from a qualified kinsman-redeemer.
5. *Complications*—the possible solution encounters obstacles at this point in the story.	5. Boaz does not have the right to redeem these women and their land, another man must be consulted.

Elements of a Skillful Plot	Representative Scenes from Ruth
6. *Climax*—the point of highest dramatic tension in the narrative.	6. The future of Ruth and Naomi is placed before the entire town. For a moment it looks as if the other kinsman will triumph, but Boaz eventually becomes the kinsman-redeemer as the widows had hoped.
7. *Denouement*—the final outcome of the story's complications.	7. Boaz is given full rights to redeem the land and the widows. He marries Ruth, and Obed is born to carry on the name of Naomi's family.

8. *The Book of Ruth contains an abundance of personal interaction between its characters. More than fifty of the eighty-four verses are dialogue. Use a Bible you can mark in to color-code each character's words. Use red for underlining Naomi's words, blue for underlining Ruth's, and yellow for Boaz's.*

This exercise helps the student visualize the story's major parts. It helps quickly identify the main characters and their roles.

9. *When you have finished underlining, review the Book of Ruth, reading only Naomi's words. Judging from her words, how would you describe this woman's personality and appearance?*

Appearance is included in this question because the years of bitterness would have had an effect on her countenance and possibly her posture.

Naomi's words will be examined more closely in chapter 7. For this question, it is only important to get a general picture of her. Her words show a progression from despair to hope to praise as the narrative continues.

10. *Read the Book of Ruth again. This time read only Ruth's words. Describe the character qualities Ruth demonstrates as she speaks.*

Ruth's speech is concise and gracious. It is important to note that her words are followed by actions. She chooses her words carefully and carries them out with commitment.

11. *During the third reading of Ruth, read only Boaz's words. How would you describe this man's personality and character?*

Boaz's words are full of references to the LORD and blessings for those he lives with. He is a man of his word. His encouragement of Ruth is filled with kindness. Yet he shows courteous assertiveness when he deals with his relative over the future of Elimelech's family.

12. *Reflect on your conversations this last week. How do your words compare with the encouraging and supportive conversations found in Ruth?*

Try to help your group members evaluate a specific dialogue they engaged in this past week. Help them discern what effect their words had on others and what character qualities these words revealed about themselves.

*13. *Consider Jesus' words, "For out of the overflow of the heart the mouth speaks" (Matthew 12:34). Prayerfully evaluate your heart's condition in relation to the words you have spoken recently.*

This passage is in the context of a run-in between Jesus and the Pharisees. These men were accusing Jesus of casting out demons with power from Satan. His answer to them is a sharp rebuke, relating that only good can come from good and only bad from bad. He continues to tell them that words are an indicator of what is in the heart of a person.

14. *Write the primary message of the Book of Ruth in your own words. Decide which scene illustrates this message.*

There are many opinions about the book's major purpose. Some of them include:

    a. Universalism—God's truth is for every race.

    b. Friendship—Ruth and Naomi's relationship is an example of true friendship.

    c. Genealogy—David's bloodline is the story's purpose.

    d. Levirate marriage—The story gives an example of the Levirate law.

Two possibilities seem to carry more merit:

    a. God's sovereignty—The book is full of God's intervention on behalf of His people. He carries the characters through times of emptiness to moments of great blessing. In every part of the narrative, He graciously works His plan for the present generation and for the generations to come.

    b. The proper use of the Law—The response of the characters, particularly Boaz, portrays going beyond the Law. He responds to the needs around him not by merely following the requirement of the Law but by carrying out the heart of it.

A dialogue that illustrates the book's primary message is Ruth 2:12. In this verse, Boaz expresses God's sovereign kindness to those who come to Him by faith.

15. *How can this message affect your present circum-stances?*

God's sovereign rule over each generation and over each person's life gives us confidence and hope for tomorrow. Naomi's despair was very real, and so is the despair of many women in your study group. But the LORD is moved by our need, and He will respond to our faith.

4

THOSE WHO KNOW YOUR NAME WILL TRUST IN YOU

Objectives

1. To discover the meanings of the people's names in the Book of Ruth.
2. To identify God's names and their meanings as used in this narrative.
3. To relate these meanings of names to the story's message.
4. To explore what God's names mean personally.

Background

The author of the Book of Ruth immediately gives us important information about the story's main characters. Four times in this book's first four verses the words "name," "named," or "names" are used. The author does not want the reader to miss the significance of this information.

Below are listed other references to the importance of names throughout Ruth:

Reference from Ruth	Description of the Naming Situation
Ruth 1:20–21	Naomi's desire for a name change.
Ruth 2:1	Boaz's name is introduced.
Ruth 2:19	Ruth shares the name of Boaz with Naomi.
Ruth 4:5	Boaz expresses the critical responsibility of perserving the name of Elimelech's family.
Ruth 4:17	The townswomen give an important name to the new child born to Ruth and Boaz.
Ruth 4:18–21	A list of important names is given to demonstrate the continuing family of God's chosen people. This list is the lineage of King David which also became the lineage of the Messiah.

Below is a list of the names in the Book of Ruth. Write the meaning you discover from a Bible encyclopedia or a Bible dictionary beside each name.

Names from Ruth	Name Meanings
Elimelech	my God is king
Naomi	my joy, my sweetness, or my pleasantness
Mara	bitter

Names from Ruth	Name Meanings
Mahlon	weakening or sickly
Kilion	failing or wasting away
Orpah	stubborn, neck, or double-minded
Ruth	friendship or something worth seeing
Boaz	swift, strength
Obed	one who serves, slave of
Jesse	Jehovah exists
David	beloved
Bethlehem	house of bread
Moab	desire or from my father

1. *How did Elimelech represent his name's meaning through his actions and decisions?*

Elimelech's choice to find provision for his family in Moab signified a departure from God's covenant. The land was tied so closely to this covenant relationship that by leaving the land Elimelech was breaking his contract with God. He was looking to another land and another king for his family's safety and security.

2. *What was Naomi expressing by asking the townspeople to change her name?*

Naomi couldn't bear the light, pleasant name she knew before leaving Bethlehem. The joy her name represented had gone from her life. She wanted to be called by a name that expressed her present bitter life.

3. *What significance might the names of Naomi's children have had on the family's decision to flee from the famine in Bethlehem?*

If Mahlon and Kilion were named because of events surrounding their births, it is possible that they were sickly babies. That they died in the prime of life further supports the possibility of poor health. If this was the case, Elimelech and Naomi would have felt desperate about doing something to save their sons when the famine spread to Bethlehem.

4. *Compare the name meanings of Ruth and Orpah. How did these Moabite women express the characteristics implied by their names?*

Orpah's decision to return to Moab can be seen as an expression of double-mindedness. She began the journey to Bethlehem and refused to turn back at Naomi's first insistence. But ultimately she must have believed that security could be found in something other than God.

Ruth's name has two possible meanings. We are told nothing directly about her personal appearance, so the name "something worth seeing," may supply the missing information. Whether or not she was beautiful, her character qualities would certainly have made her attractive. The other meaning of her name, "friendship," is expressed constantly and selflessly as she demonstrates friendship to Naomi.

5. *Boaz's name means "strength" or "fleetness." Describe the kinds of strengths (emotional, physical, or spiritual) you see Boaz possessing.*

Chapter 2 describes Boaz as a man of standing. He had wealth and responsibilities that would require physical stamina and emotional stability. In the spiritual realm, he expressed true spirituality as he generously provided for two needy widows. The swiftness implied by his name finds a perfect expression as he rushes to the city gate to attend to Ruth's request. He was a man of action.

6. *What is the name of the other kinsman-redeemer in our story? Yet what was his motive in relinquishing his rights and responsibilities to Boaz?*

How ironic that this man's fear of endangering his own estate caused him to miss the opportunity to be remembered throughout the ages. His concern for his own affairs left him nameless to readers in other generations.

7. *Explain why Ruth uses "LORD" as she expresses her commitment to Naomi and her people (Ruth 1:17).*

Ruth's knowledge of the Lord came through her association with Elimelech's family. She must have heard many accounts of how the Lord intervened in the lives of His people.

The use of this name expresses Ruth's own belief in a God who actively participates in His people's lives. She was asking this God to deal with her personally if she broke her commitment to Naomi's family.

8. *Analyze why Naomi used both "LORD" and "Almighty" as she related the events of the past years to the townspeople of Bethlehem (Ruth 1:20–21).*

By using the name "Almighty," Naomi acknowledged that the God who is sovereign over all of life's circumstances had allowed much sorrow to enter her life. The two uses of "LORD" in verse 21 may be an expression of remembering the covenant relationship with God. This covenant was broken by her family as they left the land, but she had returned to the boundaries of the agreement. Her covenant-God had brought her back to the land of promise.

9. *Why did Boaz use "LORD" when he was speaking to Ruth (Ruth 2:12)?*

Boaz realized the choices Ruth had made. She had left everything to be faithful to the LORD and His people. He was calling on his personal God to actively reward this foreign woman's unusual faith.

10. *In Ruth 4:11–15, "LORD" is used four times. Why would the elders and townspeople make use of this name in this situation?*

The marriage of Boaz and Ruth was a relationship that would preserve the name of a beloved family in Bethlehem. This covenant-God had severely disciplined Elimelech's breach of contract, but now He was lovingly restoring this family. The townspeople were calling on their covenant-God to continue renewing and blessing the family in future generations. Later (verses 14–15) they praise the LORD for hearing prayers and for answering through Obed's birth.

11. *What name do you use when addressing God? What pictures of God does this title bring to your mind?*

The most common titles used for God today are: Heavenly Father, Lord, God, Jesus Christ, Jesus, and Holy Spirit. Have your group relate the pictures or impressions a particular title creates in their minds. For example, the title Heavenly Father may give them an intimate picture of God or it may give them a formal impression of Him. Help them discover how the titles they use for God reflect their relationship to Him. Listen carefully for those who do not have a title that communicates intimacy with God. It may suggest that they are unaware such a relationship can exist.

12. *If you could give yourself a name representing the relationship you've had with God this past year, what would that name be?*

13. *If you were to analyze your present relationship with God, what name would you use for yourself?*

14. *What name do you want to possess as an expression of your relationship to Him a year from now? ten years from now?*

These three questions are designed to help your group members evaluate their relationships with God. So that each person in the class can have the opportunity to answer and discuss the questions, you may need to divide into smaller groups.

*15. *Prayerfully consult God about how you can begin expressing the characteristics of the name you desire. As you pray, be conscious of how you address Him. What are you communicating by the name you use?*

If you decide to divide into smaller groups for questions 12–14, have them remain there to close in prayer. Each small group may conduct its own prayer revolving around question 15.

5

DECISIONS, DECISIONS

Ruth 1:1–5

Objectives

1. To observe the importance of the land to God's covenant people.
2. To understand that Elimelech's decision represented a violation of that covenant.
3. To analyze personal decision-making processes.

Cultural Definition

Ephrathites—an older name meaning inhabitants of Bethlehem. The use of this aged title may suggest that Elimelech's family was an established, integral part of the community. They were probably part of the aristocracy.

Background

A famine in a land that depends on agriculture for both food and trade is disastrous. The text doesn't tell us the specific causes for the crop failure, but two options are possible. If the famine came because of lack of rain, Bethlehem's geographic location would explain the localized problem. This "House of Bread," which the word Bethlehem means, lay east of the hill country, which blocked potential precipitation. In contrast, the area of Moab that was most accessible to Elimelech received sixteen inches of rainfall a year.

The famine might also have been due to enemy raiders. Judges 6:1–6 is thought to describe the same circumstances experienced by Elimelech's family. This passage tells of foreign warriors camping near the Israelites. Whenever the crops matured, the invaders would destroy the grain and carry off the livestock. The reward of the harvest was never experienced by the Israelites.

Whatever the cause of the famine, God was disciplining His people. During Elimelech's lifetime, the Israelites were disobedient as a nation to the covenant they had formed with God. The covenant said disobedience would be punished by an impoverished land and by the rule of foreign nations. These hardships were not to destroy the Israelites but to cause them to repent and return to their God. By running to green pastures in Moab, Elimelech was avoiding the spiritual issue behind the famine in Israel.

Examining Elimelech's Decision

1. *If you had discussed with Elimelech whether he should go to Moab or stay in Bethlehem, what pros and cons would you have considered?*

PROS	CONS
There is no food in Bethlehem. Moab has plenty.	We are leaving everything and everyone we have ever known.
The boys are already sickly, they could never survive the diseases that accompany famine. They need all the nutrition we can provide.	God has spoken about our involvement with the Moabite people, we are not to seek security from them.
Our nation is experiencing political instability, so it might be good to leave until things get a little more stable.	The Moabites may reject us. We are dependent on their hospitality if we cross their borders.
God's covenant with my forefathers included the land—I wonder if I really believe that anymore.	God's gift to our family is the land we live on—how can we ever leave it?

2. *How long did the family plan to stay in Moab (Ruth 1:1)? About how long did they stay (Ruth 1:4)?*

The family was only intending to stay in Moab "for a while." In actuality, they stayed more than ten years. How often that happens to *temporary* situations and decisions.

3. *Review God's instructions to His people concerning Moab (Deuteronomy 23:3–6). Why do you think Elimelech disregarded these specific prohibitions?*

When your own children are dying and enemy raiders are at your back door, the first impulse is to run to safety. To stand by and wait for God to act when you can run to fertile fields is an immense test of faith. Elimelech ran to the immediate "sure thing," but that situation soon turned to heartache and sorrow.

In this era of Israel's history, the Law was not esteemed or frequently read in public. Therefore, it is possible that Elimelech was ignorant or forgetful of God's instructions concerning Moab.

4. *List the family's original purposes for moving to Moab. Compare this list with the consequences of their move.*

Original Purposes for Moving to Moab	Consequences of Moving to Moab
To save the family.	The head of the household dies.
To make sure the sickly children survive.	Both sons die.
To ease the hardship for Naomi.	Naomi becomes a childless widow, a serious plight in those days.

5. *What significance did the land hold for the Hebrew people (Genesis 12:1, Deuteronomy 4:1)?*

God was not only dealing with an individual when He made His covenant with Abraham. He was also committing Himself to a nation. Part of the provision and promise for that nation was the land that God would provide for their daily needs. Because the land was part of the covenant, it was used to register God's approval or disapproval of His people's spiritual temperature.

6. *What statement was Elimelech making to God when he crossed the border into Moab?*

Many views are held about the significance of Elimelech's decision and his death. Below is one assessment of the situation. You may wish to read it to your study group and ask for responses of agreement or disagreement.

> Elimelech left the people of God and the geographical boundaries of the blessing of God. In doing so he was in effect denying the meaning of his name. He was rejecting the rule of God in his life. In an understandable concern for the welfare of his family (both sons seemed to be unlikely of surviving infancy), Elimelech did a rash act: He left the land, he abandoned his people, he walked away from his God. In this act (which should be understood as a breach of covenant during a time of divine discipline), Elimelech was guilty of a capital crime. He was judged with death. Not only he, but also his sons died in the land of Moab. Naomi is correct when she lays these deaths at the hand of God (Ruth 1:20–21). The *torah* was serious; it dealt with ultimates. Serious breach meant serious judgment.

> —Dr. Ronald B. Allen
> Professor of Old Testament
> Language and Exegesis at Western
> Conservative Baptist Seminary

Deuteronomy 1:19–36 gives insights into the hearts of those who refused to receive the provision of this land years before Elimelech.

7. *Why did God allow the Promised Land to experience famine during Elimelech's lifetime? (See Leviticus 26:3–5, 14–20.)*

The bounty of the land was an expression of God's approval. Famine in the land signaled God's displeasure with the people's hearts and actions. The blessing of the land was

God's reward for their obedience, and the curse of the land was their punishment for disobedience.

> 8. *Judges 6:1–6 records the circumstances that some believe coincide with the Book of Ruth. Why does it say these events were happening?*

The Israelites were once again doing "evil in the sight of the Lord." His discipline included oppression by the Midianites who destroyed their crops and livestock, and even drove them from their homes. This constant pillage combined with inadequate rainfall would have created an exceedingly desperate situation for Elimelech's family and the entire community of Bethlehem.

Examining Our Own Decisions

> 9. *Identify one of the most difficult decisions you have encountered in the past.*

> 10. *Where did you go for counsel about the decision?*

> 11. *How did you find relief from the tension and anxiety caused by the decision?*

> 12. *Would you do anything different if you had a second chance?*

Questions 9 through 12 help each group member evaluate her process of decision making. Often the sources used for counsel and the places sought for relief from anxiety reveal a person's spiritual health. Reflecting on the past may recall the heartache of a choice specifically prohibited by God, or it may identify a choice that was consistent with His will. Whatever the decisions have been, learning from them for future choices is invaluable.

> 13. *Think of a decision you are facing now and list any Scriptures that give you insight into what you should do. If you feel there are no specific scriptural instruc-*

tions that address your situation, try this: Search for passages that give insight into the attitudes you are to exhibit during the evaluation of this decision.

Many times directions for specific decisions are not given in Scripture; i.e., which house to buy, where to go to college, whether or not to change jobs. In these cases, it is important to focus on who we are to be during the decision–making process. Refocusing of anxiety (Philippians 4:6–7), financial contentment (Hebrews 13:5), and keeping in step with the Spirit (Galatians 5:26) are just a few of the instructions that can guide us in daily decisions.

14. *If you find you need to take a specific action or to change an attitude in response to the Scriptures you have examined, record how you plan to participate in the changing process.*

It is not enough just to agree with God that change is necessary. We must also agree to cooperate with Him in the changing process. This cooperation could include anything from emotional desire to physical action. Help your group form specific, measurable goals in answer to this question.

15. *God's people encounter suffering for reasons other than making wrong choices, what are these other reasons as indicated in the following passages: James 1:2–4; 2 Corinthians 1:3–11; Deuteronomy 8:1–5.*

God allows hardship to enter our lives for many reasons. Under each Scripture reference is a brief summary of the reasons we suffer.

James 1:2–4

> to test our faith.
> to develop in us the quality of perseverance, which leads
> to maturity and completeness in our lives.

2 Corinthians 1:3–11

    to experience God's comfort.

    to be skilled in comforting others.

    to promote patient endurance in our lives.

    to help us learn to rely on God instead of ourselves.

    to cause the giving of thanks to God, who sees us through the difficulty.

Deuteronomy 8:1–5

    to humble us.

    to purify our hearts.

    to strengthen our obedience.

    to train us as a father trains his children to become mature and ready for the challenges of life.

    to increase our dependency on God.

6

YOUR GOD SHALL BE MY GOD

Ruth 1:6–18

Objectives

1. To examine what prompted Orpah's return to Moab.
2. To discover what actions Ruth took to follow through on her stated commitment to Naomi.
3. To evaluate the fulfillment of personally stated commitments to others.

Cultural Definitions

Levirate marriage—Naomi's argument in Ruth 1:11–13 contains a reference to the Hebrews' Levirate law. This law, recorded in Deuteronomy 25:5–10, makes provision for a widow by requiring her brother-in-law to marry her. The law's purpose was to provide an heir for the dead husband to continue his name through the generations of the Israelites. The first son from this Levirate marriage was considered the child of the

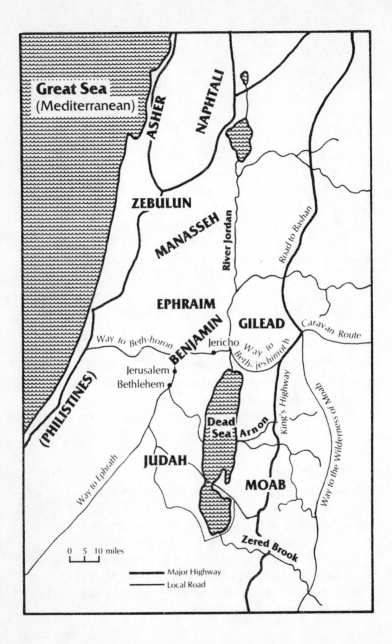

widow's first husband. This child bore the name of the deceased man and became full heir to his estate.

Naomi's argument is that she is too old to bear sons who might fulfill the law's requirement by marrying Orpah and Ruth. She also argues that even if she could bear sons, the daughters-in-law would have to wait too long for their Levirate marriages.

Background

Leaving Moab to return to Judah did not mean calling the travel agent and booking the next flight to Bethlehem. The journey that lay ahead of these women was long and tedious.

The Book of Ruth does not tell us the exact route taken by Naomi and Ruth. It only says they "set out on the road that would take them back to the land of Judah" (Ruth 1:7). We can only speculate about their route by examining the major highways and local roads in existence at that time.

To the east of the travelers lay Moab's wilderness. To the west, travel was blocked by the Dead Sea. The Wilderness of Edom and the Desert of Arabah lay to the south. The only option left was a northern trip along the King's Highway. This route was considered a major roadway, but it can hardly be compared to our interstate highways of today. It would more closely resemble the roads followed by American pioneers.

After traveling north, the women needed to veer west and might have taken the local road called the Way to Bethjeshimoth. The next possible leg was through Jericho and was called the Way to Beth-horon. To reach Bethlehem to the south they might have taken the Way to Ephrath, which passed through Jerusalem and on to Bethlehem.

The "highway departments" in those days only worked on special occasions. During wartime the roads were smoothed to promote the efficient travel of warriors. The only other time the roads received attention was when royalty took a journey. The servants of a king would go before the royal caravan, filling in the ruts and removing large stones.

The donkey caravan was the most common means of travel in Ruth's day, but it is doubtful that these two widows would have owned a donkey. So it is probable that they traveled by foot, walking approximately ten miles a day.

The distance of the journey was probably between fifty and sixty miles, depending upon how far Elimelech's family migrated to Moab's interior. This means the trip lasted about one week if the two women were able to cover ten miles each day.

Because rain made the roads nearly impassable, the best time of the year to travel was during the long, hot, dry summer. And it appears that Naomi and Ruth's arrival in Bethlehem was during the early part of this dry season, at the beginning of the barley harvest.

The roads were dangerous places during the period of judges because the oppressive Canaanites molested and stole from all who traveled. Deborah's song in Judges 5:6 indicates that travelers took the side roads, and the major highways became almost abandoned. It took great courage for two women to begin the long journey alone. Maybe their obvious poverty was a blessing as they trudged arm in arm along the rutted, treacherous roads to Bethlehem.

Naomi's Logic

1. *Explain the major points of Naomi's argument for her daughters-in-law to return to Moab (Ruth 1:8–15).*

Major Points of Naomi's Argument

a. *"Go back to your mother's home."*

The two Moabite widows had close relatives who could provide for them in their own country. Naomi had no idea what faced her in Bethlehem. These two young women had their entire lives ahead of them. They should remain where the future was "secure."

b. *"May the LORD show kindness to you . . ."*

Here Naomi extends a blessing to her faithful daughters-in-law. She prays that the true God will continue to touch their lives even as they return to a land where Chemosh, the local deity of the Moabites, is worshiped.

c. *"May the LORD grant that each of you will find rest in the home of another husband."*

Marriage was the only career open to women in this era. Naomi knew her young daughters would easily find other husbands in their native land, but the men of Bethlehem would hesitate to consider foreign brides.

d. *"Am I going to have any more sons who could become your husbands?"*

This statement refers to the Levirate law defined at the beginning of this lesson. Naomi clearly shows that she is too old to provide husbands for Ruth and Orpah through the birth of more sons. Naomi has no way of providing for the younger women, but their homeland would hold hope for the future.

e. *"It is more bitter for me than for you, because the LORD's hand has gone out against me!"*

This argument refers to the discipline experienced by Elimelech's family because they left the Promised Land. Naomi wants these Moabite women to get on with their lives. They had no initial part in this fatal family decision, but they had been deeply affected by it. Naomi doesn't want them to experience any more heartache because of Elimelech's family.

2. *Why do you think Orpah chose to return to her homeland? What did she gain by reappearing at her Moabite mother's home? What did she lose by saying good-bye to her Israelite mother-in-law?*

Orpah listened to logic; it made sense to return to Moab. She also listened to the suggestion as coming from an older, respected woman. Her decision was anything but impulsive. It is important to remember that she also wept and promised to stay with Naomi, which was an unusual act for a foreign bride. As the arguments continued, she kissed her beloved companions good-bye and returned to the only place that made any sense.

Orpah's Gain

—a secure future

—the opportunity to remarry in a familiar culture

—the possibility of having children

—the comfort that accompanies the familiar

Orpah's Loss

—the companionship of two women who had shared her sorrows

—God's abundant blessing in Judah

—the opportunity to know God in depth through association with His people

Ruth's Commitment

In the table below, you will find two columns. The left column contains each aspect of Ruth's classic expression of commitment. The right column is to be filled with the actions Ruth took to express her pledge to Naomi. Use the entire Book of Ruth to find the ways Ruth remained true to her promises.

The Promises	The Practical Expressions of Commitment
3. Where you go I will go.	Ruth walked every step of the tedious journey back to Bethlehem. She was willing to head toward uncertainty.
4. Where you stay I will stay.	The lodging of the two women when they reached Bethlehem is unknown. All we know is the poverty they experienced. Ruth took the initiative despite their circumstances and sought to alleviate some of the suffering by gleaning.
5. Your people shall be my people.	Ruth willingly married a foreign man when the two women were settled in their new home. She chose to bear a son that would continue the name of Naomi's family. When this child was born, Ruth let the women of another nation name him. She truly was letting Naomi's people be her people.
6. Your God shall be my God.	Ruth purposely left a land where Chemosh was worshiped and joined the Israelites in revering Yahweh. She was willing to conform to the laws and customs practiced in honor of Yahweh.

The Promises	The Practical Expressions of Commitment
7. Where you die I will die, and there I will be buried.	Aborting her decision and going back home was not an option for Ruth. She initiated gleaning to provide for their immediate needs and she accepted a marriage that would provide for their future needs. This commitment was not only for Naomi's lifetime. Ruth was taking God and His people as hers for her lifetime as well.
8. May nothing but death separate you and me.	Ruth pledged to care for Naomi the rest of her mother-in-law's life. Ruth brought this woman into her home when she married Boaz. Ruth also allowed her to care for the child who would carry on the family name. No options existed for the separation of these two women except death.

Our Personal Commitments

9. *What spoken commitments have you made to other people in your life? They may have been the simple but profound words, "I love you." They may have been the words we use too lightly such as "I'll pray for you." Whatever those words are, see if you can state them in*

the table below and evaluate the ways you have actively expressed your commitment.

Verbal Commitments	Practical Expressions of Commitment

Encourage discussion by asking group members to share one item from their charts. The ways some have expressed their commitments may help others with creative options.

10. *Maybe you discovered a commitment that you have not maintained consistently. Maybe you cannot continue that commitment; if so, share your withdrawal of commitment so the people involved are not left wondering. If you want to continue the commitment, list it below and choose one action you will take this week to live out your promise.*

Depending on the transparency between group members and the size of your group, you may wish not to discuss this question, or you may discuss the frustrations they feel when they do not fulfill their commitments. If you choose to discuss possible actions for unmet commitments, allow time at your next meeting for reports of attempted projects.

11. *How many people or causes can we commit ourselves to in the same way Ruth committed herself to Naomi? Explain your answer.*

Very few. Ruth's kind of commitment demanded her entire life; it called for many sacrifices. For us to follow through with this level of commitment, other priorities must be set aside. It is realistic to say most people could only handle one relationship with this kind of commitment.

12. *Name the things that cause you to hesitate before you commit yourself to another person.*

This question is designed to help your group understand the commitment needs of each other. Some women may be very anxious to give and receive commitments of deep friendship. Others may feel overcommitted and unable to establish new, close friendships. Because of these different needs, some women may register coolness, and others may register warmth. By communicating individual commitment levels within the group, you will be avoiding misunderstandings that could hamper the atmosphere of your study time.

*13. *What commitment level do you have toward the other members of your Bible study group? How have you expressed your commitment?*

Not every member of your group will be able to strongly commit herself to the study group. Some women may have other priorities that take precedence over the relationships within the group. However, it may trigger some thinking about what each person can contribute as well as what they want to receive from the group.

As the leader of this lesson or of the entire study, use this question for your personal barometer. What do you feel your commitment to the group should be? How can you express this as you prepare and as the group meets together?

This question is designed for personal meditation—not group discussion. You may want to close this lesson by asking God for wisdom as each woman sorts through her commitments. If some commitments need closer attention, others must be dropped. Pray for discernment to know the difference and courage to carry out the change.

7

TRANSFERRED SPIRITUALITY

Ruth 1:19−22; and all the dialogues involving Naomi.

Objectives

1. To evaluate Naomi's character by examining her conversations with others.
2. To analyze Naomi's spiritual influence on Ruth.
3. To sharpen personal skills in communicating and modeling spiritual truth to others.

Background

Ruth 1:3 gives an immediate clue that Naomi is prominent in this story: Elimelech is described as her husband, which is an unusual designation in a patriarchal society. It signals that Naomi will be a major character.

In Ruth 1:19−22, one of the first things we learn about Naomi is that she asked for a name change. This request expresses the bitterness-pleasantness theme that weaves its way through the book. Her words, "I went away full, but the

LORD has brought me back empty," represent two scenes at these city gates. The past scene was one of fullness for Naomi as she had a husband, two sons, and material possessions. The present scene is one of bitter emptiness; her family is dead, and she is destitute.

But, even though Naomi does not know it, the second scene is not the last. The narrative continues with another scene at the city gates. In this third moment, God restores Elimelech's family by providing a kinsman-redeemer. Naomi had gone out full, and the Lord had brought her back empty. But He will restore her.

Despite the deep pain Naomi experienced over her losses, she faithfully modeled two critical concepts before the people around her:

a. Awareness of God's involvement in life's details.

b. Selfless concern for those closest to her.

Analyzing the Qualities of a Remarkable Woman
Dialogue #1—Ruth 1:8–15

1. *What primary concern did Naomi's words communicate?*

Naomi knew the adjustments of leaving one's homeland. She had emigrated ten years before, but then she had left with hope for a better life. These two women are planning to leave their homes with no future hope or security.

Naomi is refusing to put those she loves through such uncertain circumstances. She is willing to lose the last two members of her family if it means a better life for them.

2. *Through her concern, what attribute was Naomi modeling despite her poverty and heartache?*

To be able to consider the welfare of others in the midst of one's overwhelming grief is an unusual display of selflessness. Naomi knew she would experience loss once again if her daughters-in-law returned to Moab, but she thought of their future instead of her own hurt.

Dialogue #2—Ruth 1:20–21

3. *How bitter was a widow's life in Old Testament times? (Look up "widow" in a Bible encyclopedia.)*

It is interesting that the two Hebrew words used for widow in the Old Testament actually mean "silent one" and "one bereaved." No options were open to widows in this period of history except remarriage. Naomi's situation was especially hard because of the death of her children and her age, which prevented a second marriage.

Many commands throughout the Old Testament are directed toward meeting widows' needs. Some of the instructions were given to counteract mistreatment of these vulnerable women. The Old Testament prophets frequently evaluated a nation's spirituality by the treatment it gave widows (Isaiah 1:23). The Psalms also portray God as the defender of the fatherless and the widow (Psalm 146:9). They were to receive compassion and extra care.

4. *In Ruth 1:21 Naomi says, "The Lord has afflicted me." What is your reaction to Naomi's words?*

At first glance it appears that Naomi is blaming God for His cruelty toward her. However, because of the name she uses for God (see lesson 4) and because of her character, there could be another possibility. She might have been saying:

> God, with whom I have a covenant relationship, has intervened in my life with disciplinary actions. He is mighty and cannot be toyed with. Because we left the land of promise and broke our covenant with Him, we have suffered greatly. God has allowed us to experience the fruits of our disobedience. I am bitter. I hurt, and I am

more discouraged than at any other time in my life. But I still call Him my covenant Lord. I went away, but He is bringing me back to the land of promise.

5. *What aspects of God's character was Naomi relating to the townswomen in front of Ruth?*

Naomi was describing the difficult circumstances that had made her life so sorrowful, but she did not attribute them to fate. In answer to the question of her identity (verse 19), she expressed God's personal involvement in her life. She used God's personal, covenant name and His mighty, sovereign name. She was expressing the balance between His awesome sovereignty and His tender intimacy.

She was also saying that God and His laws are not to be taken lightly. When His covenant is breached, His holiness demands discipline and justice. He is not to be taunted or tested. Disobedience does not escape His notice. He deals firmly and thoroughly with it.

Dialogue #3—Ruth 2:19–22

6. *What attitude did Naomi communicate to Ruth about those who showed kindness to them?*

Naomi was not too proud to welcome kindness. She humbly desired that the one who had much, while she had little, might be blessed even more by God.

7. *What part of God's character did Naomi express to Ruth in verse 20?*

Hope began to return to Naomi's bitter life. She does not say, "Well, Ruth, we've finally pulled ourselves up by our own bootstraps." Instead, she attributes this surprise abundance to a kind and faithful God.

8. *Describe the feelings Naomi communicated about Ruth's new job in verse 22.*

Ruth was a foreigner trying to assimilate a new culture. She knew no one and worked alone in fields filled with people who had no reason to have respect for a Moabite. She was an easy, defenseless target for ridicule and harm. Naomi was relieved to know that she had been promised protection. Once again Naomi expresses a concern for Ruth's welfare.

Dialogue #4—Ruth 3:1–4

9. *Restate in your own words the reason Naomi gives for this detailed planning session.*

Verse 1 gives the reason for the planning session. The word Naomi used for "home" means rest or security. Naomi wanted to see Ruth cared for and settled in life. Marriage was the only avenue of security for women in this historical period.

Naomi and Ruth were taking mutual responsibility for each other's needs. Ruth had gleaned through the entire harvest season to put a little food on their table. Now Naomi was taking the initiative to provide a more permanent solution to their plight.

10. *In this passage, what attribute was Naomi modeling for Ruth?*

With this tangible plan, Naomi was again demonstrating a selfless concern for her daughter-in-law. Ruth was assured in word and deed that Naomi loved her.

Modeling Spiritual Truth to Others

11. *Who has had the most influence on your spiritual development? Explain what that person has done or said to make you hunger for a deeper knowledge of God.*

Try to allow time for each person to explain her answer to the question. This sharing will help the group become familiar with one another's spiritual journey. It may also provide creative ideas for influencing others.

12. *List the people you influence each week. How are you modeling true spirituality to them?*

Emphasize the importance of living a consistent spiritual life in front those under one's own roof. Genuine love and concern for one another is one of the strongest evangelistic tools outlined by our Lord in John 13:35. Naomi's relationship to Ruth is an example to us of this priority. We need to be modeling spirituality where it is usually the most difficult—at home.

13. *Choose one person from your list and develop ideas of how you can effectively attract him or her to Christ or how you can strengthen that person's relationship with God.*

Reemphasize the two major ways Naomi communicated her faith:

1. Verbally testifying to God's character.

2. Modeling selfless concern for those closest to her.

*14. *If you have a mother-in-law and/or daughter-in-law, evaluate your relationship with her. What can you do to improve your relationship so that it begins to resemble the commitment between Ruth and Naomi? (If you do not have in-laws, use the same evaluation of mother/daughter or aunt/niece relationship.)*

Close this lesson with a time to thank God for the model Ruth and Naomi's relationship gives women today. Invite the group members to specifically thank God for the mothers-in-law and daughters-in-law He has placed in their lives. Pray that commitment and transferral of spiritual truth might characterize those relationships.

8

A KNIGHT IN SHINING ARMOR

Ruth 2:1–23

Objectives

1. To evaluate how Boaz's lineage may have affected his actions toward Ruth.
2. To observe the creative ways Boaz met Ruth's needs.
3. To make an appraisal of Boaz's character based on the way he obeyed God's law.
4. To analyze your personal obedience level to the heart of God's commands.

Cultural Definitions

Gleaning—The Hebrew word means to pick up or gather up. This activity took place during the harvest seasons. As the owners of the land gathered in their crops, some of the produce was missed. In Leviticus 19:9 and 23:22, landowners are required to leave what the reapers missed for the poor and the foreigner.

Barley Harvest—This harvest began about a month ahead of the wheat harvest in Bethlehem. The heads would ripen and be ready for gathering near the end of April or the first of May.

Roasted Grain—This dish was prepared by gathering choice ears of barley or wheat and tying them into small clumps. These bundles were then placed over a hot fire and roasted. The grain was then enjoyed as grits.

Ephah of Grain—An ephah was a common dry measurement used in Old Testament times. It was equivalent to about one half of a bushel.

Lineage of a Hero

1. *Read Tamar's story in Genesis 38. This story was probably passed down through the generations, and it is likely that Boaz had been told of the episode from which his ancestor Perez had been born. What influence might this story have had on Boaz's response to Ruth and Naomi?*

Tamar's story involves the issue of the Levirate marriage. She was a childless widow with a father-in-law who wanted to escape the requirements of the Levirate law. In her desperation, she initiated an unorthodox plan that would solve her childlessness. Judah was caught accusing her of ungodliness while he himself had been partner in the act. He had refused her right to his sons in marriage, and she had taken the matter into her own hands.

Boaz may have known this story well. If so, he chose to learn from the mistake of his forefather. When Judah was faced with a widow's needs, he chose to disobey God's law that provided for these despairing women. When Boaz was faced with Ruth and Naomi's needs, he went beyond the law to make sure their needs were met.

2. *Read Rahab's story found in Joshua 2:1–24 and 6:24–25. Because of possible exclusions from the genealogies in Ruth and in Matthew, we are uncertain whether Rahab was Boaz's mother or grandmother. In either case, she was well known to Boaz. How might this relationship between Rahab and Boaz have affected Boaz's view of Ruth?*

This Gentile woman has the distinction of being included in God's Hall of Faith in Hebrews 11. Her welcoming of the spies in Jericho was considered an act of faith. The Book of James commends her for believing in Israel's God and showing loyalty to His people.

Prejudice toward foreigners ran high in Israel during the period of the judges, but Boaz would have had an edge against prejudice because of his close relationship to Rahab. When the stories of Ruth's faith circulated through Bethlehem, Boaz must have been interested. Foreign blood flowed in his veins, and he was in a unique position to accept the sincere faith of someone outside Hebrew biological ties. He would also have had a heightened sensitivity toward the dependency of a foreigner on Israelite kindness. His overwhelming kindness to Ruth at their first meeting indicates an unusual concern for the alien.

A Close Look at Our Hero

3. *The entrance of Boaz into our story immediately changes the depressing picture of Ruth and Naomi's poverty. In his first encounter with Ruth, he carefully and sensitively meets her needs. Use the entire chapter to identify Ruth's needs and Boaz's creative provisions. Record your findings in the table:*

Ruth's Needs	Boaz's Provisions
Physical:	
v. 8–9 protection from other workers	He encourages her to stay with his workers and instructs his men not to lay a hand on her.
v. 9 thirst	He invites Ruth to drink from the water that has been drawn and guarded for his workers.
v. 14 hunger	He invites Ruth to eat the same thing he and his workers are eating. He not only gives her a little for herself but he also gives her enough to take home to Naomi.
Emotional:	
She was in need of encouragement and kindness in this new land among new people with different customs.	Boaz encouraged her with praise for her sacrifice shown through caring for her mother-in-law.
security	Boaz gave her the guarantee that she could continue to work in his fields all though the harvest season. She knew she would not have to look for gleaning in other fields where she might not be welcome.

Ruth's Needs	Boaz's Provisions
Spiritual:	
Life was very difficult for Ruth and Naomi in Bethlehem. Ruth probably needed renewed confidence that Yahweh would care for her in a personal way.	Boaz asks a blessing from Yahweh upon this Moabite woman. As he asks this in Ruth's presence he reminds her that because she came seeking Him, He truly will reward her. This encouraging reminder of Yahweh's personal involvement in all of life must have given Ruth renewed strength to continue gleaning day after day.

4. *What did the law require Boaz to do for the poor and the foreigner who came to glean in his fields (Leviticus 19:9; 23:22)?*

Boaz was under no obligation to extend extra kindness to those who might glean in his fields. His only requirements by the law were to leave the crops missed by his harvesters and to leave the edges of the field unharvested.

5. *How would you evaluate Boaz's obedience to this requirement of the law?*

Boaz went beyond duty as he related to Ruth; he didn't stop at mere obedience to the law. He saw past the provision for the poor in general to one poor woman who had many needs—many that he could personally meet. As the table shows, he was very sensitive to the physical, emotional, and spiritual needs of this foreign woman who had chanced upon his field.

6. *List all the things Boaz did that were not required by the letter of the law.*

He gave Ruth his own food to eat at mealtime.

He spoke kindly to her.

He let her glean among the sheaves.

He gave her water to drink.

By granting these extra privileges, he gave her the same status enjoyed by his own workers.

7. *What does Boaz's level of obedience demonstrate about his character?*

The period of the judges was a time in Israel's history when few people cared about God's laws. It is suspected that after years of famine, landowners were not allowing the poor to glean the fields. Boaz was not only an example of one who obeyed God's command to leave grain for the gleaners but also one who went beyond the command. During the harvest, the reapers came first to cut the barley, followed by the workers who bound the stalks into sheaves. Only after the sheaves had been carried off the field were the poor allowed to glean. But Boaz allowed Ruth to glean among the harvesters and commanded them to leave loose stalks on the ground for her. This passage demonstrates Boaz's protection, generosity, and compassion.

A Close Look at Ourselves

8. *Read James 2:1—13. What is the requirement for relating to the poor today?*

This New Testament passage commands us to show no favoritism to the rich. It states that a person's economic position should not determine the degree of honor and respect he or she is shown. The demonstration of these qualities should come from an understanding of the worth

God places on each individual. In addition, this passage notes that many times it is the poor who are rich in faith.

9. Prayerfully evaluate how your personal actions and attitudes measure up to these instructions.

This question may be used to lead the members of the group in a discussion of situations in which they showed favoritism or in which they received favoritism. Expressions of favoritism may not be as blatant as the one described in James, but any expression reveals the same problem. Also, have the group share personal experiences of how they have seen poverty or deprivation build faith.

10. *The letter of these instructions is: Do not show favoritism. What do you think the spirit of the command is (James 2:8)?*

"Love your neighbor as yourself."

11. *Describe a situation in which you observed someone else expressing the spirit of this command to the poor.*

This question gives your group an opportunity to hear creative ways others have been sensitive to those less fortunate than themselves. See if you can get them to think globally as well as locally.

12. *How can you go beyond lack of favoritism to loving the needy as yourself this week? Review your table on pages 55–56 for some creative ideas from Boaz.*

Encourage specific actions and words from the women. Your group may even want to engage in something together. Sharing experiences and projects like this can enhance relationships in your study group.

9

INITIATORS BEFORE A SOVEREIGN GOD

Ruth 3:1–18

Objectives

1. To examine how each main character participated in solving Ruth and Naomi's problems.
2. To understand that human participation is an important part of God's sovereign plans.
3. To correctly initiate solutions to current personal difficulties.

Cultural Definitions

Threshing floor—The location of the threshing floor was determined by exposure to a wind that would aid in the winnowing process. Once the location was determined, the ground was carefully prepared. A circular area was first cleared of loose stones. Then the ground was moistened, tamped, and swept. Animal-drawn sledges would then begin the threshing by raking over the harvested grain. After the grain was raked, it was thrown into the air with wooden forks. This winnowing process was done during the late afternoon when a strong breeze appeared. The wind blew away the lightweight chaff as the heads of grain fell to the ground.

Spread the corner of your garment over me—This term is still used in many Eastern cultures to mean marriage. It is often symbolically performed in marriage ceremonies by the bridegroom, who places a cloak around the bride. Ezekiel 16:8 also uses the term as it describes the covenant relationship between Yahweh and Israel, using the marriage imagery. Ruth was asking Boaz very directly to marry her. This was an unusual circumstance because women did not normally propose in Hebrew culture. Boaz had not taken the initiative because another kinsman had rights before him.

Gift of Grain for Naomi—As Ruth left the threshing floor in the early morning hours, Boaz sent her away with a gift for her mother-in-law. These six measures probably refer to seahs, which were about one-third of an ephah (⅜ to ⅔ of a bushel). The gift Boaz helped to position on Ruth's head could have weighed more than eighty pounds. It was intended for Naomi because she was in a position to grant permission for the marriage. This gift was a much greater amount than Ruth was able to glean in a day and shows how, with Boaz, the widows' needs would be abundantly supplied.

Initiating a Solution to Ruth's Need

1. *Naomi's first words in chapter 3 could also be expressed this way: "I feel responsible to see you settled in life. I want you to be well cared for." What factors from the story made it the right time for Naomi to pursue a better life for Ruth?*

Some possible factors:

a. With the harvest completed, Naomi and Ruth had lost their ability to support themselves.

b. Naomi was growing older with each season and might have felt an urgency to provide a secure future for Ruth.

c. Enough time had passed for Ruth's character to dispel any national prejudice that might have made it awkward for an Israelite man to marry her.

d. It is likely that Boaz himself did not guard the grain every night. Somehow Naomi had discovered that this was his night on duty.

2. *What do Ruth's words in verse 5 reveal about her appraisal of Naomi? What kind of a person could you say those words to?*

In order to obey someone completely, complete trust is needed. Ruth had been through a lot of hardships with Naomi. She trusted the older woman to perceive the best solution to their situation.

3. *How does Ruth introduce herself in verse 9? What is she expressing by the identification she chose to use?*

Ruth's identification as "your servant" communicates two things to Boaz. First, she is expressing humility. Second, she is reminding him of the status he gave to her the first day she gleaned. He had shown her unusual preference and had let her enjoy the same privileges as his servant girls.

4. *What is the meaning of her request, "Spread the corner of your garment over me?" (You may want to check a commentary or look at Ezekiel 16:8 where the same phrase is used.)*

Background material for this idiom is found under Cultural Definitions at the beginning of this lesson.

5. *What is she communicating in the last phrase of her petition, "since you are a kinsman-redeemer"?*

Because Boaz was related to Naomi's husband, these women had a right to ask him for help. Ruth wanted to make it clear that her approach for help was for proper reasons. She was also emphasizing that they had no other hope except through the intervention of a kinsman-redeemer.

6. *Boaz's response in 3:10–11 gives us a wealth of information about Ruth. Make a list of these insights:*

Verse 10a—Boaz's reference to "my daughter" may represent the age difference between the two.

Verse 10b—Ruth was faithful to her family responsibilities instead of pursuing her own desires. Boaz seems to refer to a definite group of young men. Apparently, Ruth could have had other suitors if she had wanted them. This compliment acknowledges Ruth's attractiveness.

Verse 11—Boaz knew that Ruth had been watched and appraised by all the townspeople. He agreed with their conclusion that she was a woman of noble character. He told her not to be afraid, because her virtue had won her honor. He would commit himself to meet her needs.

7. *In this narrative the vow that usually receives all the attention is Ruth's commitment to Naomi in chapter 1. However, in Ruth 3:13 another vow is made that deserves equal attention. What impact would this reply have made on Ruth?*

Boaz vows with the words, "As surely as the Lord lives." He is communicating to Ruth that she can have complete confidence in him. She had trusted the LORD, and He had proven faithful. Now she could trust Boaz to meet her need with the same faithfulness.

8. *At the close of the threshing floor scene, Boaz performs two acts on Ruth's behalf. Record those acts and describe their significance to Ruth.*

Verse 14—Boaz had Ruth leave the threshing floor before anyone could recognize her. He wanted to protect her reputation. Ruth had conducted herself virtuously, and he didn't want anyone to think otherwise.

Verse 15—Boaz gave Ruth a gift for the head of her household. He wanted to communicate his commitment to meeting the needs of the entire family.

9. *What does Naomi tell Ruth to do next (verse 18)? How do you feel when this is the only thing left to do?*

In our society we are not used to waiting, and we want instant everything—instant solutions to our problems and instant relief from our discomfort. Naomi is telling Ruth that they need to stand by now and entrust someone else with their need. They have done all they can, and it is time to relinquish the responsibility and wait.

10. *Each of these main characters has expressed his or her devotion to a sovereign God in the previous chapters. By word or deed they have also demonstrated belief in His interventions and His involvement in their lives. However, in chapter 3, they all seem to take matters into their own hands—or do they? The table below contains four references that record the contributions made toward solving the widows' dilemma. Fill in the table by identifying the characters and their contributions.*

Character	Contribution	Reference
Naomi	creative planning	3:1–4

Character	Contribution	Reference
Ruth	complete obedience	3:5,9,14–15
Boaz	committed action	3:10–13,15; 4:1
Naomi & Ruth	confident waiting	3:18

Initiating Solutions to Our Needs

11. *When should you initiate solutions to your personal needs, and when should you stand by and let God do something without your intervention?*

12. *If you decide to initiate action, are you opposing belief in a sovereign God? Explain.*

In dealing with these questions, one of the key issues to address is our creation in the image of God. We were made to be people of creativity and choice. As we express these qualities, we reflect the image of God in a unique way. Naomi knew that in God's law, help for the poor was the responsibility of a kinsman-redeemer. Her plan was a creative way to ask for that help. Ruth obeyed God by faithfully living each day with honesty, virtue, loyalty, and kindness. Boaz honored God by responding wholeheartedly to a need he had the power to meet.

All of these characters help us to see that belief in a sovereign God does not deny choice, creativity, action, or initiative. Our Lord has invited us to participate in His sovereign plans. We share His Word, and others are saved. We give of ourselves, and others are encouraged. We pray, and He allows us to participate in the changing of hearts and lives. As we initiate *godly* action in the face of needs, we do not deny Him but rather reflect Him.

*13. *Identify a difficulty you are presently facing. Put your name by the stage of the solution process you are in. Write out how you will participate in this stage.*

Name	Solution Stages	How I will participate
	creative planning	
	complete obedience	
	committed action	
	confident waiting	

Sometimes it is difficult to evaluate the part we can play as we face personal needs and the needs of others. We can't always participate in all four stages of the solution process. But this chart may give your group members new hope as they evaluate their participation in solving the needs they currently face.

10

A DAY IN COURT

Ruth 4:1–10

Objectives

1. To understand the Hebrew concept of redemption.
2. To compare the qualifications of Boaz and the close relative to redeem Elimelech's land and care for his relatives.
3. To evaluate Jesus Christ's qualifications to be our Redeemer.

Cultural Definitions

The city gate—Most Palestinian cities were fortified by rock or brick walls. The main entrance to the city was a large gate that several people could pass through at a time. Because of the common use of the gate, it was considered the civic center of town—news was shared, gossip exchanged, and legal matters settled.

Because the homes were within the city walls and the fields were outside the walls, Boaz could be certain that the relative he needed to speak with would pass through the main gate in the morning.

Ten elders of the town—It is possible that this number of elders is significant to the story. Ten was the number of elders required to pronounce the marriage blessing. However, it is not certain that this custom was observed as far back as the period of the judges. If it was, Boaz was obviously preparing for more than a land transaction.

Taking off the sandal—This formality is not to be confused with the custom described in Deuteronomy 25:7–10. The latter custom is a retaliation for a brother refusing to fulfill his duty in the Levirate marriage. The custom exercised in Ruth 4:7–8, is the finalization of rights being transferred to another. By taking off his sandal, the nearest kinsman was relinquishing his rights to Boaz.

Background

Naomi's forced land sale mentioned in Ruth 4:3 was not uncommon in Hebrew communities. Many Israelites found themselves lacking during the period of the judges. According to Hebrew law, relatives were required to help maintain the family inheritance by buying back a poor man's land. If the Israelite became so poor he had to sell himself, then the relatives were required to buy back his freedom.

God's other provision to alleviate the sorrows of poverty was the Year of Jubilee. After working the land six years, the Israelites were wisely instructed to leave the land fallow the seventh year. Each of these seventh years was called a sabbatical year. After six successive sabbatical years, the seventh one was called the Year of Jubilee. According to Leviticus 25:28, 40–41, land previously sold because of poverty was returned to the original owner for free and people previously sold were given their freedom without a price.

Both of these provisions, redemption and Jubilee, demonstrated God's priority of family loyalty and His compassion for the poor. The heart of these laws, given during the theocratic rule of Israel, is reiterated in the New Testament as James tells us that true religion is demonstrated in such practical ways as caring for widows and orphans in their times of great need (James 1:27).

The Background of Redemption

1. *What instructions had God given His people concerning the redemption of land (Leviticus 25:23–25)?*

The Israelites were to remember that the land was the Lord's. He was master of it, and they were His tenants. Because of this relationship, the land could not be sold permanently. If the poor had to sell their land, their relatives were responsible to buy it back—to redeem it.

2. *How were these instructions obeyed in the Book of Ruth?*

Naomi still had rights to the land Elimelech possessed before the family left for Moab. When she returned to Bethlehem, her poverty made it imperative that she sell the land. Boaz used proper legal channels to meet this need of his relatives. He offered the land to the man who possessed legal first rights, but he was also prepared to fulfill the responsibility if the closer relative was unwilling.

3. *Read Leviticus 25:47–55 carefully. What instructions had God given concerning the redemption of people?*

Some of the Israelites became so poor that they only had themselves left to sell. Because they were the Lord's servants, they still possessed the right to be redeemed. Close, prosperous relatives were responsible to restore their brother to freedom.

4. *After Boaz approaches the nearest relative with Naomi's forced land sale, he brings up another issue. What did God require of the widow's family (Deuteronomy 25:5–6)?*

The law mentioned in Deuteronomy 25:5–6 is the law of Levirate marriage. If the dead man had no children, his brother was required to marry his widow. The first child of this marriage would be considered the heir of the dead brother and would be entitled to any inheritance the deceased man may have acquired. The extinction of a family name was a terrible tragedy in Hebrew culture, so this law was to continue the lineage of a man who had died with no heirs.

5. *Neither Boaz nor the close relative was Elimelech's brother. (Boaz's reference to "our brother" in verse 3 means a larger circle of relatives.) Because they were not brothers in the same household, the letter of the law did not require them to marry Elimelech's widow or his son's widow. What appeal does Boaz use for Ruth's marriage (Deuteronomy 25:6b; Ruth 4:5)?*

Boaz saw past the law's minimal requirement and helped his relative see that they were responsible to carry on Elimelech's name. Boaz put a premium on family loyalty and said Elimelech's name must be continued even as his land must be redeemed.

6. *From Ruth 4:4 to 4:6, the closest relative has a change of heart. Why do you think he relinquished his rights to Boaz?*

The closest relative found this redemption responsibility a danger to his own estate. We are left to speculate concerning his specific reasons. It is possible that he was already married and did not want two wives. It is also possible that he did not want his child through Ruth to be called the son of Mahlon. Whatever his reason, this man, who was so concerned about preserving his own name, is left unnamed in the story of Ruth.

The Qualifications of a Redeemer

7. *If the closer relative is held up beside the qualifications of a redeemer, where does he fall short?*

Qualifications	The Unnamed Relative
a. He must be a close relative.	a. 3:12—he was the closest relative to Ruth and Naomi.
b. He must perform the redemption willingly.	b. 4:6–8—he was unwilling or unable to take on the redemption responsibilities.
c. He must possess the price of redemption.	c. 4:6—he could be indicating an inability to take on the triple responsibility of buying the land, caring for Ruth and Naomi, and letting the land be the future possession of Ruth's son.
d. He must be free himself.	d. 4:6—it is obvious that he is a free man by his referral to his own estate.

8. *How does Boaz compare with the same list?*

Qualifications	Boaz
a. He must be a close relative.	a. Ruth 2:1,20; 3:2 and 3:9 all speak of the family ties between Boaz and Elimelech. Ruth 3:12 raises the problem of a man more closely related to the two women. This is resolved when the relative relinquishes his right to Boaz before the town elders.
b. He must perform the redemption willingly.	b. Boaz shows not only willingness (Ruth 3:11,13) but also eagerness (Ruth 3:18) as he meets the needs of his relatives.
c. He must possess the price of redemption.	c. Boaz is introduced in the narrative as a man of prestige and wealth (Ruth 2:1). Ruth 4:9 tells us he purchased everything that had belonged to Elimelech.
d. He must be free himself.	d. Boaz's wealth and prestige confirms the fact that he was a free man. His possession of servants also indicates that he was the free master of his household (Ruth 2:8,15).

Is Christ Qualified to Be Our Redeemer?

9. *Evaluate Jesus Christ the same way the close relative and Boaz were evaluated. Is Jesus qualified to be our Redeemer? Use a concordance to find Scriptures supporting Christ's ability to redeem. Look first at the New Testament entries under the following words: "redeem," "redeemed," "redeemer," and "redemption."*

Qualifications	Jesus Christ
a. He must be a close relative.	a. Through the birth of Jesus Christ, God became flesh and dwelt among humanity. As true God and yet true man, Jesus identified completely with our humanity and is qualified to be our close relative (John 1:14; Hebrews 2:14; 2:17).
b. He must perform the redemption willingly.	b. Philippians 2:5–11 expresses Christ's willingness to be our redeemer through his obedience even to the point of death. His submission to the Father on our behalf expresses the infinite love he had for us. He was willing to pay for our costly redemption with His own life.

Qualifications	Jesus Christ
c. He must possess the price of redemption.	c. In I Peter 1:18–19 we are told that our redemption was secured not by money, but by the blood of Jesus Christ. Our redemption is therefore incorruptible and nothing on this earth can reverse or destroy it. The cost of our redemption is to be one of the motivating factors for living holy lives (1 Corinthians 6:19–20).
d. He must be free himself.	d. Christ was the only one who knew true freedom from sin and death. 1 Peter 3:18 describes Him as the just (one not condemned by the law because He perfectly fulfilled it) who died for the unjust. In John 8:31–36 Jesus is explaining to the Pharisees the impact of the freedom he can provide. He states that a son has authority in his father's house to give or withhold freedom. The conclusion to be drawn is that Christ, the only Son of God, has the unique authority to give true freedom to man.

10. *What difference does it make to know that Jesus Christ is qualified to provide for your redemption and eternal life?*

Your group may include members who have never realized their need for Christ's redemption. Use this time to allow them to express their questions and thoughts about this basic but profound foundation in our relationship with God.

If your entire group has accepted redemption through Christ, use this time to worship God by sharing with each other how much this act means.

*11. *Use the last moments of your study time to review the chart of Christ's qualifications as a Redeemer. Tell your Kinsman-Redeemer how you personally feel about the costly price he paid for your spiritual life and freedom.*

You may want to follow up this personal meditation time with a group prayer thanking God for the redemption He provided through Jesus Christ.

11

A TIME TO RESPOND

Ruth 4:11–17

Objectives

1. To observe the townspeople's response to the completed redemption.
2. To parallel Ruth's response to Boaz with our responses to our Kinsman-Redeemer.
3. To encourage community praise in response to the events of life.

Background

Ruth's first encounter with Boaz caused her to respond by bowing to the ground. He was a land owner and an Israelite; she was acknowledging his cultural superiority and humbly expressing her amazement at his kindness.

In chapter 4, Ruth is elevated to a place beside Boaz as his wife. Poverty and want are over for Ruth and Naomi. The time of emptiness is past; now a time of fullness begins. This story, which started mournfully with three deaths, ends in celebration with three births. Faith, commitment, and generosity have borne fruit.

These concluding verses resound with the townspeople's responses. They are honoring God for His involvement in the events of life, and they are praying for the people they have come to love and respect.

A Time to Bless

1. *As the townspeople respond to the redemption, they ask the Lord to make Ruth like Rachel and Leah. Why do you think they chose these two women?*

Ruth 4:11 describes these women as the ones who "built up the house of Israel." They were the wives of the patriarch Jacob. Between the two of them and their servants, twelve sons were born, who became the fathers of the twelve tribes of Israel. The townswomen were expressing desire that Ruth be a fruitful mother.

2. *The townspeople also ask a blessing for Boaz. To understand the significance of their words, remember that the Levirate marriage was a sacrificial act of concern. How might Boaz have felt when the townspeople spoke the words found in Ruth 4:11b?*

What an encouragement these words must have been to Boaz. The townspeople were well aware of the sacrifice he was making. The other kinsman had reminded everyone that this commitment could jeopardize one's personal estate. After years of famine, this added responsibility would be costly for Boaz.

A Time to Respond

Questions 3 through 7 have two parts. The first part of each question relates to Ruth's response to Boaz. The second part provides an opportunity to evaluate personal responses to God. The answers below are added information for the first part of the questions. The second part will be answered subjectively and individually by your group members.

3. *In Ruth 2:10, what did Ruth's actions and words express about her character?*

Ruth knew these kindnesses were not usually extended to poor, foreign women. She was responding to Boaz's mercy by bowing before him in humility.

Bowing is not customary in Western culture. What would it mean to you if you observed someone bowing with his or her face to the ground in response to God's undeserved kindness? Do you feel comfortable in this prayer posture?

4. *How does Ruth respond in 2:13?*

Ruth praised Boaz for the kindness and comfort he had provided for her.

What expressions of comfort and kindness has God directed toward you recently? Have you acknowledged these before Him with thanksgiving?

5. *In Ruth 2:14, Ruth doesn't greet Boaz's offer for food with a polite, "No thank you; I'm just fine." What is she expressing by receiving his provisions?*

Ruth knew she was dependent on Boaz's kindness. She acknowledged her need by receiving what he offered her.

How self-sufficient are you? Do you go it alone in your spiritual life, or do you agree with God's appraisal of your need by receiving His provisions, i.e. wisdom from His Word, comfort through the Spirit, strength through prayer?

6. *In Ruth 3:9, we find our humble responder doing some bold initiating. Why was this action appropriate?*

Ruth had a desperate need, and Boaz could meet that need. It was appropriate for her to approach a man qualified to redeem Elimelech's family. She was asking not just for herself but for the sake of the family name.

The proposal might have been made secretly to give Boaz the freedom to say yes or no. Ruth's private initiative also allowed Boaz to take the public initiative later on.

> We are needy before God, and He has invited us to come to Him with our cares. How often do you exercise this privilege as God's child?

7. *What is Ruth expressing by her response to Boaz in 3:13—14a?*

When Boaz instructed Ruth to lay at his feet until morning, she followed his instructions explicitly. By her obedience, she was trusting Boaz to handle the threshing floor meeting.

> When you come to understand instructions through God's Word, how complete is your obedience? How complete is your trust in God?

A Time to Celebrate

8. *The townswomen attending the shower did something unusual; they named the child (verse 17). What is the meaning of the name they gave? What significance does the name have for Obed's position in the family?*

"Obed" means servant. The townswomen were naming him for the servant role he would play in these two widows' lives by inheriting Elimelech's land and by carrying on the family name.

9. *As the townswomen speak in verses 14—15, their words reflect the components of true celebration. Can you identify the components?*

   a. Verse 14a—Praise to God for works He has done on behalf of His people.

   b. Verses 14b–15a—Prayer for future blessing and hope through this new child.

   c. Verse 15b—Honor to the one who has been faithful to God and His people.

10. *Are these components evident in the events you celebrate in your family, in your church, or among your friends? Which ones are included? Which ones are missing?*

You may want to encourage your group to analyze the type of celebrating they are familiar with by discussing a specific holiday or occasion. You could have them relate how each of these factors is included in their Christmas celebration. Have them recall the last baby shower they attended. What was included in the celebration of a birth?

11. *Building traditions around remembering God's faithfulness to your family builds strong relationships between those who have shared the occasion. How can you incorporate these celebration components in your next family holiday?*

Have each group member write down the next celebration she will be planning. Help them decide how these elements can be joyously included in their festive occasions.

You may also want to point out that each family may have special events in the past that show God's faithfulness. It would be appropriate for these occasions to be celebrated even if they are not national holidays.

12

WILL I ALWAYS FEEL THIS EMPTINESS?

Ruth 4:18–21

Objectives

1. To observe the restoration the Lord brought to the land and to His people in the Book of Ruth.
2. To see God's faithful, sovereign plan worked out in individual lives and in Israel's corporate life.
3. To be encouraged by looking at God's sovereign purposes being worked out in our lives.

Background

If you begin adding up the years from Perez to King David, you may wonder how so few men's lives could cover more than eight hundred years. Hebrew genealogies do not always include each person within the line. The genealogy at the end of Ruth is thought to mention only the names of the the clan's well-known members. It is also possible that the genealogy contains an important symmetry, with five fathers named from the Egyptian sojourn and five fathers chosen from the Exodus to the Kingdom Age. Despite the fact that some names may have been omitted, this genealogy gives us the needed links to family lines. It is also the only detailed lineage given in the Old Testament for David, one of Israel's greatest kings.

The Cycles of Emptiness and Fullness

1. *Using the following table, compare the land's condition with the story line. Beside each reference describe the plight of the land and the plight of the characters at that point in the story.*

Reference	Condition of the Land	Condition of the People
1:1–5	Famine, infertility.	Death, grief, barrenness.
1:6–22	Fruitfulness—the harvest is about to begin.	A returning to the homeland, a faint glimmer of hope.
2:1–23	The harvesters are gathering the abundance of the land.	Ruth brings home an abundant provision for the poverty of the two widows—hope begins to grow.
3:1–4:21	The harvest is over. Food has been provided for the hungry and the surplus is stored for security in the coming years.	Boaz takes Naomi and Ruth into his home for their protection and provision. Ruth bears a child that ensures the continuity of Naomi's family line and provides hope for

Reference	Condition of the Land	Condition of the People
		coming generations.
		Future security and hope for the nation of Israel is seen by the inclusion of King David in the genealogy.
		This lineage also points to the line through which the Messiah would come —the One who is the hope of the entire world.

2. *Throughout the story, both the land and the characters experience a cycle from emptiness to fullness. This second table helps you trace this theme through the narrative.*

Emptiness ·		Fullness	
Record the destitute circumstances found in the following verses.		List the *references* and *incidents* that resolve the former times of emptiness.	
1:1–4	The destruction of famine, death, and poverty.	1:22	The land is fertile again. The barley harvest can begin.
		2:14–18	Kindness is shown through Boaz as he provides physically for Ruth and Naomi.
1:11–13	Naomi has no hope for a husband and must face the barrenness of old age.	2:20	A possible kinsman-redeemer shows interest.

Emptiness		Fullness	
		2:22	The land has been fertile; the barley harvest can begin.
		3:10–13	A vow of help is obtained from a qualified kinsman-redeemer.
1:20–21	The complete emptiness of Naomi is expressed through her desire to be called Mara.	4:13	Ruth is married to Boaz and gives birth to a baby boy.
		4:16	Naomi's arms are filled with the child who will carry on the name of her family.

The Unchanging God

3. *In Ruth 1:13 and 1:20–21, Naomi describes her life's most difficult season. Even at her deepest moments of loss, what did she possess?*

Naomi's loss was overwhelming, but she had not lost everything. God had left her with a faithful companion, an option to return to her homeland, and the unchanging promises He had given to His people of whom Naomi was a part.

4. *Compare Naomi's seasons of fullness with her season of emptiness. How many years did she know emptiness? What parts of her life were years of fullness?*

Naomi describes her life before Moab as full. Since the sojourn in the foreign country was approximately ten years, we can estimate that it was almost twelve years from entering Moab until Naomi held Obed in her arms. Twelve years is a long time to bear heartache and to know poverty, but it is not forever. God had allowed difficult times to touch Naomi's life, but He had also worked restoration and blessing back into her aching heart.

Many women in your study group may be experiencing heartaches and difficulties. God may have entrusted some with sorrows and hurts that have continued longer than Naomi's. They may desperately need someone to come alongside and help bear their burdens as Ruth did with Naomi. Encourage your group not only to be ones who study together but also ones whose practical love for each other is a witness to our impersonal world.

5. *Naomi and Boaz testify to the same aspect of God's character in Ruth 1:8 and 2:12. How can this part of God's character be a comfort in times of trial?*

Naomi and Boaz testify that God does not forget a person's kindness and faith. Frequently, in the midst of suffering, it becomes difficult to remain faithful and believing. We grow weary with doing good, and we become impatient to see what is unseen. We want to see the eternal fruits of our labors—NOW! What a comfort it is to know that He remembers and rewards our faithfulness.

> Therefore we do not lose heart. Though outwardly we are wasting away, yet inwardly we are being renewed day by day. For our light and momentary troubles are achieving for us an eternal glory that far outweighs them all. So we fix our eyes not on what is seen, but on what is unseen. For what is seen is temporary, but what is unseen is eternal.
>
> —2 Corinthians 4:16–18

6. *Compare the first time the* LORD *is mentioned in the Book of Ruth (1:6) with the last time (4:14). What aspect of God's character does He demonstrate through*

these actions on behalf of His nation and of one individual?

God is a restorer. He must express His justice, but His mercy moves Him to respond to His people's repentent cries. The period of the judges is full of God's merciful acts on a national level. In the Book of Ruth, the land's restoration is an expression of God's gracious forgiveness of Israel.

His intervention on behalf of Elimelech's family demonstrates His mercy on an individual level. He brings restoration to Naomi's life when He fills her arms with a precious baby boy who will carry on the name of those she lost so tragically in Moab.

7. *What message for the nation is contained in the genealogy in Ruth 4:18–21?*

This genealogy does not just signify the continuation of a biological line. It demonstrates the continuation of God's faithfulness to each generation of His people. Each father mentioned had a different relationship with God. Some were faithful, some were not. The first father, Judah, leaves much to be desired in the area of spiritual maturity (Genesis 37:26; 38). In contrast, the last father of the lineage is King David, who was called a man after God's own heart (Acts 13:22). Despite the ups and downs of the human heart, God is unchanging and eternally faithful to His people.

8. *With what man does the genealogy conclude? What was the spiritual tenor of his life (Acts 13:22)? What was his contribution to Israel (2 Samuel 3:17–18)?*

David, son of Jesse, was anointed as Israel's second king. The two best known events of his life are the slaying of Goliath and the adulterous relationship with Bathsheba. He had moments of victory and moments of failure, but despite the ups and downs, his life and reign were characterized by obedience and love for the Lord. He led many victories as the Israelites battled their surrounding enemies, and he initiated a great period of national praise and worship.

9. *This same genealogy appears in the New Testament (Matthew 1:3–6). What man is the focus of this genealogy? Describe his life's significance.*

Matthew's genealogy traces Jesus Christ's kingly line. He is the Promised One, the Messiah that had been anticipated through all the generations listed in this passage. Through the years, God was faithfully carrying out His promise to provide a Savior for the world.

Three significant Gentile mothers, Tamar, Rahab, and Ruth, are included in this list. Their faithful acts were rewarded by inclusion in the lineage of the Savior of Jew and Gentile alike.

The Seasons of Our Lives

Many times in the Psalms, the writers remember God's faithfulness to gain confidence for a present difficulty. This exercise is designed to encourage a similar kind of remembering in our own lives. The sorrowful seasons and the joyous seasons are both to be recorded. God's sovereign work in our lives and the lives of others is being accomplished through hardship and blessing.

Date	Seasons I have Experienced	God's Sovereign Work

10. Use the last moments of your study time to thank God for the ways He worked through the empty and full times in Ruth and Naomi's lives. Use the chart above to thank Him for His work in your personal life. Then identify the present season you are experiencing and renew your trust in His sovereign control.

As you remain faithful to Him during each season of life, may you be richly rewarded by Yahweh, the God of Israel, under whose wings you have learned to take daily refuge.

Pray that your group will find new courage to face difficulties as they remember God's past expressions of love and faithfulness. You may wish to lead your group in a time of praise at this final study. Try using songs or choruses that express God's sovereignty and faithfulness. Intersperse the singing with thanksgiving prayers for the things He has done in individual lives.

BIBLIOGRAPHY

Barber, Cyril J. *Ruth: An Expositional Commentary*. Chicago: Moody Press, 1983.

Cundall, Arthur E. and Leon Morris. *Judges and Ruth: Tyndale Old Testament Commentaries*, ed. D.J. Wiseman. Downers Grove: InterVarsity Press, 1968.

Enns, Paul P. *Ruth: Bible Study Commentary*. Grand Rapids: Zondervan, 1982.

Lewis, Arthur H. *Judges, Ruth: Everyman's Bible Commentary*. Chicago: Moody Press, 1979.

McQuilkin, J. Robertson. *Understanding and Applying the Bible*. Chicago: Moody Press, 1983.

Rauber, D.F. "The Book of Ruth" in *Literary Interpretations of Biblical Narratives*, ed. Kenneth R. Gros Louis with James S. Ackerman and Thayer S. Warshaw. Nashville: Abingdon Press, 1974.

Ryken, Leland. *The Literature of the Bible*. Grand Rapids: Zondervan, 1974.

Tenney, Merrill C., ed. *The Zondervan Pictorial Encyclopedia of the Bible*. Grand Rapids: Zondervan, 1975, 1976.